j
599
Lio
c.3

All about Wild Animals

LIONS

Please visit our web site at: www.garethstevens.com
For a free color catalog describing Gareth Stevens Publishing's
list of high-quality books and multimedia programs, call
1-800-542-2595 (USA) or 1-800-387-3178 (Canada).
Gareth Stevens Publishing's fax: (414) 332-3567.

Library of Congress Cataloging-in-Publication Data

All about lions.
    Lions.
       p. cm. — (All about wild animals)
       Previously published in Great Britain as: All about lions. 2001.
       ISBN 0-8368-4185-9 (lib. bdg.)
       1. Lions—Juvenile literature. I. Title. II. Series.
    QL737.C23A24   2004
    599.757—dc22   2004040811

This edition first published in 2005 by
Gareth Stevens Publishing
A World Almanac Education Group Company
330 West Olive Street, Suite 100
Milwaukee, Wisconsin 53212 USA

This U.S. edition copyright © 2005 by Gareth Stevens, Inc. Original edition copyright © 2001 by DeAgostini UK Limited. First published in 2001 as *My Animal Kingdom: All About Lions* by DeAgostini UK Ltd., Griffin House, 161 Hammersmith Road, London W6 8SD, England. Additional end matter copyright © 2005 by Gareth Stevens, Inc.

Editorial and design: Tucker Slingsby Ltd., London
Gareth Stevens series editor: Catherine Gardner
Gareth Stevens art direction: Tammy West

Picture Credits
Tony Stone Images — Tim Davis: 7, 14–15; Renee Lynn: 9, 16, 17 bottom; Peter and Stef Lamberti: 11; Michael Busselle: 13; Manoj Shah: 14; Kevin Schafer: 17 top, 27 bottom; Stuart Westmorland: 18; Mark Petersen: 20, 21; J. Sneesby and B. Wilkins: 22; Art Wolfe: 23, 24; Patricia Doyle: 26 top; Daniel J. Cox: 26 bottom; Shaun Egan: 27 center, 28; Nicholas Parfitt: 28.

All rights reserved. No part of this book may be reproduced, stored in a retrieval system, or transmitted in any form or by any means, electronic, mechanical, photocopying, recording, or otherwise, without the prior written permission of the copyright holder.

Printed in the United States of America

1 2 3 4 5 6 7 8 9 08 07 06 05 04

All about Wild Animals

LIONS

Gareth Stevens Publishing
A WORLD ALMANAC EDUCATION GROUP COMPANY

Lion Facts

Animal group: mammal

Color: tan with white underbody

Size: 8 to 9 feet (2.4 to 2.8 meters) long and 3 feet (1 m) tall at shoulder

Weight: Males weigh from 330 to 420 pounds (150 to 190 kilograms), and females weigh from 270 to 400 pounds (122 to 182 kg).

Speed: A lion can run up to 37 miles (60 kilometers) per hour for a short time.

Eats: meat

Drinks: water

Lives: In the wild, males live about 12 years, and females live as long as 18 years. In captivity, lions live up to 30 years.

CONTENTS

A Closer Look 6

Home, Sweet Home 10

Neighbors 12

The Family 14

Life in the Pride 18

Favorite Foods 20

Danger! 22

A Lion's Day 24

Relatives 26

Humans and Lions 28

Glossary 30

Index 32

Words that appear in the glossary are printed in **boldface** type the first time they occur in the text.

A Closer Look

Lions, along with tigers, leopards, and jaguars, belong to a group of animals called the big cats. Lions are among the biggest of the big cats. An adult lion is about as tall as a child but weighs as much as 420 pounds (190 kilograms), or more than two adult humans! A lion is large, but it is not slow, especially when it is hungry. To catch its **prey**, it can run as fast as 37 miles (60 kilometers) an hour, but only for a short distance.

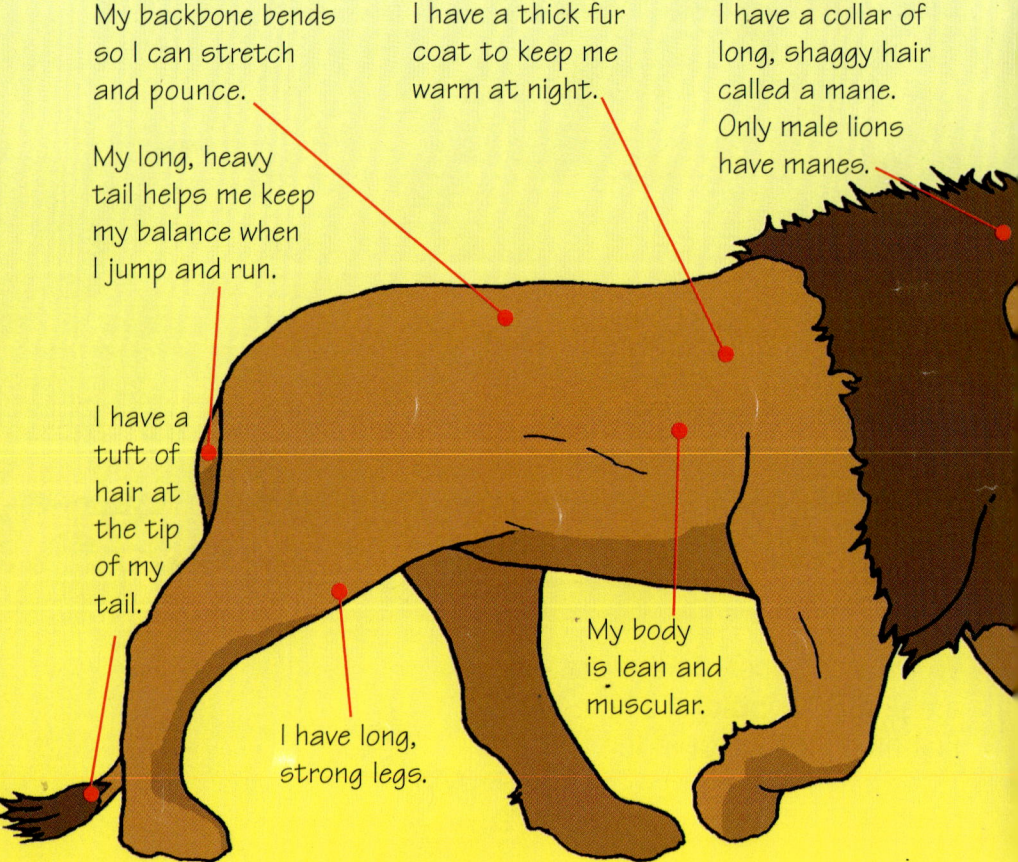

My backbone bends so I can stretch and pounce.

I have a thick fur coat to keep me warm at night.

I have a collar of long, shaggy hair called a mane. Only male lions have manes.

My long, heavy tail helps me keep my balance when I jump and run.

I have a tuft of hair at the tip of my tail.

My body is lean and muscular.

I have long, strong legs.

DID YOU KNOW?

- A lion's paw can be 5 inches (12 centimeters) wide, four times wider than the paw of a pet cat.

- Thick pads on a lion's paws help it sneak up on its prey without making a sound.

- A lion has four claws on each back paw and five claws on each front paw. Its fifth claw works like a thumb to help a lion grip things.

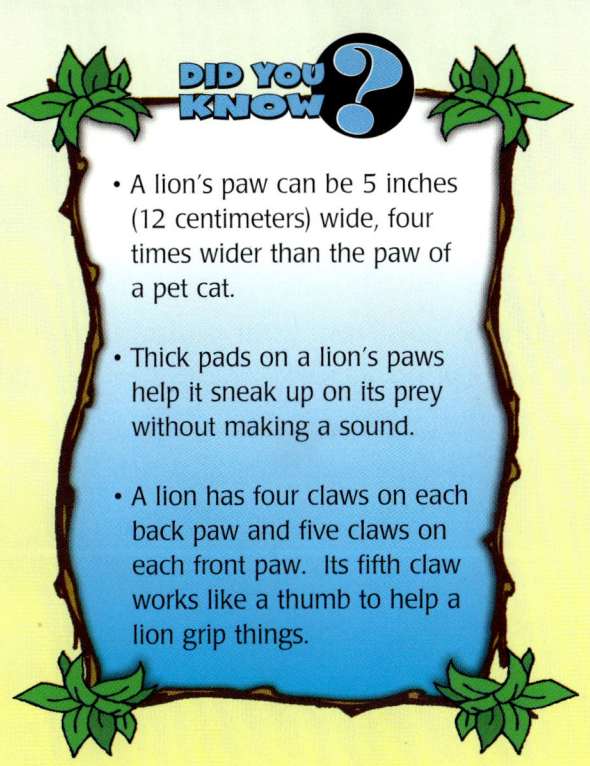

I have a big head and strong jaws that can crunch through bones.

My paws have strong, sharp claws for tearing up meat.

TWIST AND BEND

All of the members of the cat family have special backbones that twist and bend. Their flexible spines help cats jump and land smoothly.

Lions have large, round heads and rounded ears. They have good eyesight in the day or night. In the dark, lions see about six times better than humans see. They have a good sense of smell and keen hearing, which helps them hunt their prey. Lions use their pointed front teeth to stab their prey and kill it instantly. Male lions have thick, long manes, which make them look stronger. Manes help lions scare away enemies and protect themselves during fights.

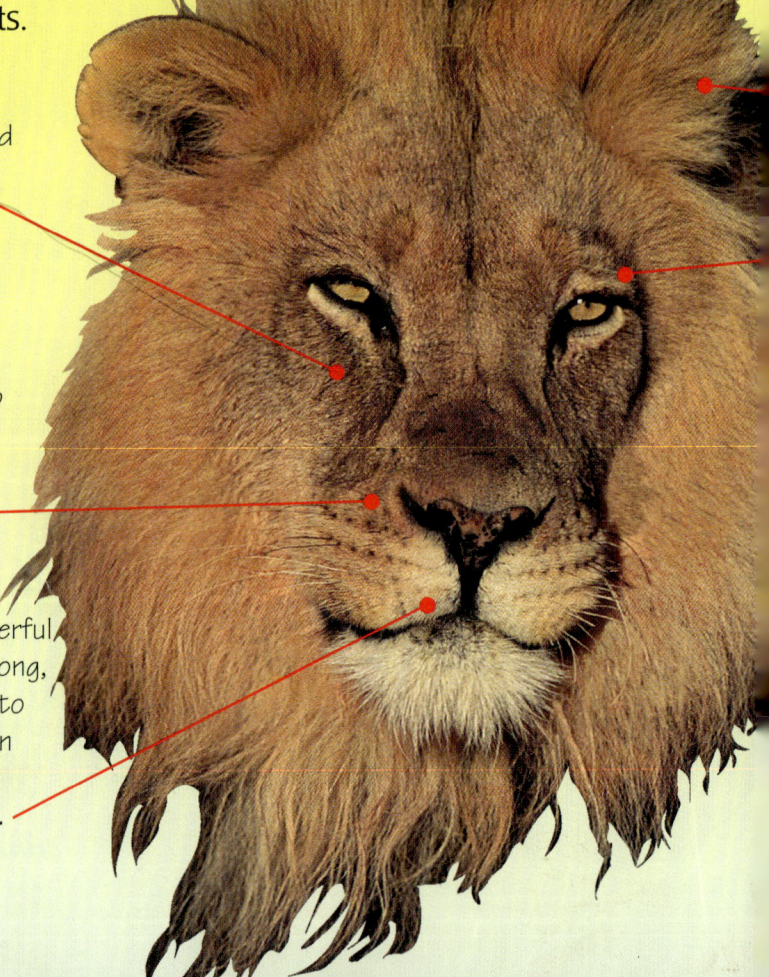

I have a round head and a short face.

My sensitive whiskers help me feel my way around in the dark.

I use my powerful jaws and strong, sharp teeth to kill prey. I can break a bone with one bite.

OPEN WIDE

Adult lions have thirty teeth, but they do not use them to chew their food. Their teeth are made for killing prey and tearing meat into big chunks. They can swallow big chunks of meat whole because they have special jaws that help them open their mouths extra wide.

The front teeth tear off chunks of meat.

Back teeth crunch bones and skin.

Long, sharp teeth stab and kill prey.

My short ears can hear quiet sounds.

My eyes are widely spaced, so I can see things to the side as well as in front of me.

WASH DAY

A lion's tongue is covered with tiny, sharp **spines**. A female lion, called a lioness (*right*), uses her tongue like a comb to gently clean the fur coat of her **cub**. When the lioness eats, she uses the spines on her tongue to scrape meat off the bones of her prey.

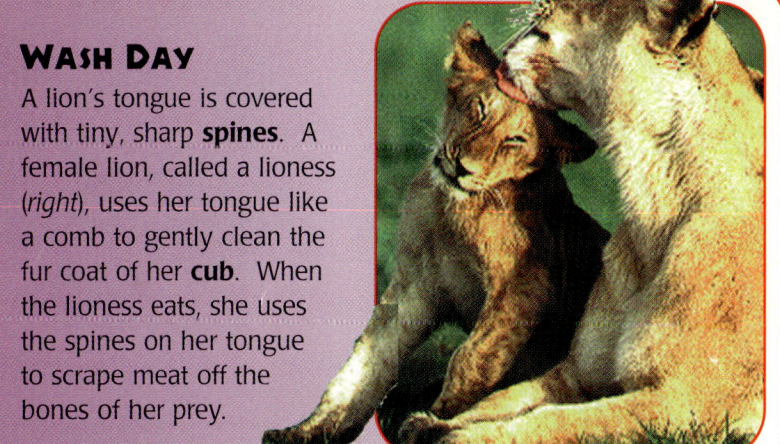

9

Home, Sweet Home

Almost all of the wild lions in the world are African lions. They live in areas of dry grassland called savannas. The weather on a savanna is warm all year, but there are two seasons — the wet season and the dry season. During the wet season, it rains almost every day, and the grass grows as tall as a person. During the dry season, it does not rain at all, and the grass dries up and turns yellow. Only trees that do not need much water, such as **acacia** and **baobab** trees, can survive on the hot, dry savanna.

Where In The World?

Ten thousand years ago, lions roamed all over Europe, Asia, and Africa. As few as one hundred years ago, many lions lived in parts of the Middle East and India. Today, only a few hundred Asiatic lions are left in India. Most of the wild lions in the world are African lions, and most of them live in places where they can be protected from humans.

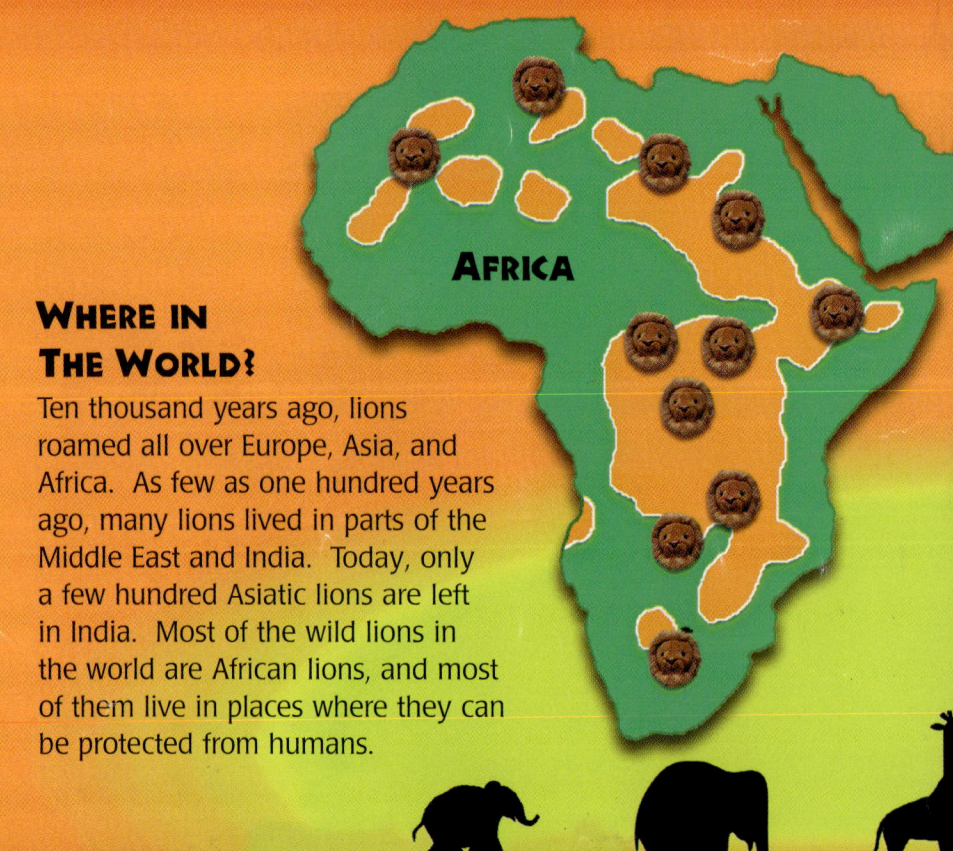

DID YOU KNOW?

The people who live in different parts of Africa have different ways to say the word "lion." Here are a few:
- *simba*, in the Swahili language used in East Africa
- *ngatia* or *muruthi*, in the Kikuyu language in Kenya
- *odum*, in Nigeria
- *ambess*, in Ethiopia

LURKING LION

The fur of lions is a purr-fect color to blend in with the grass of the savanna. When lions hunt, they hide in the long grass until they can leap on their surprised prey.

Neighbors

Many different kinds of animals live side by side with lions on the savanna. Billions of insects crawl in the grass and make tasty meals for spiders, scorpions, and lizards. Birds swoop down to catch bugs, snakes, and rodents, such as mice and ground squirrels. Herds of zebras, wildebeests, and **gazelles** roam the savanna searching for grass and shrubs to eat. Lions share the savanna with other fierce **carnivores**, such as leopards and hyenas.

Striped Hides

Most animals on the savanna have patterns such as stripes, spots, or patches of color on their fur. Some patterns make it hard to see an animal in the grass. Other patterns help one animal blend in with the rest of the herd. Patterns provide **camouflage** from enemies.

FOOD FOR ALL

Animals that eat plants are called grazers. Many grazers live on a savanna, but they do not fight over food. Each kind of grazer eats a different kind of plant or a different part of a plant. Wildebeests, gazelles, zebras, and warthogs feed on grass, but they eat different parts of the stem. Rhinos and antelopes eat bushes. Elephants and giraffes both eat leaves on trees, but only the giraffes are tall enough to reach the treetops!

WHO LIVES ON THE SAVANNA?

MEAT-EATERS
Hyenas, leopards, cheetahs, baboons, lions, and wild dogs

GRAZERS
Gazelles, elephants, giraffes, wildebeests, springboks, antelopes, rhinoceroses, warthogs, meerkats, and zebras

BIRDS
Eagles, bee-eaters, hornbills, ostriches, buzzards, hawks, and vultures

REPTILES, RODENTS, AND HARES
Snakes, lizards, ground squirrels, mice, and hares

ARACHNIDS AND INSECTS
Scorpions, beetles, termites, locusts, ants, and spiders

The Family

Most members of the cat family, such as tigers, live alone. Only lions live in groups, called prides. A pride includes about fifteen lions — from four to twelve females and up to six males. All of the females in a pride are related to each other, but the males grew up in different lion prides. At times, the lionesses may divide into groups of three or four females, while the males live in a separate group. A lioness leaves the pride before her cubs are born and does not return until her cubs are a few weeks old. Female cubs stay with the pride their whole life, but males must leave when they can live on their own. Each pride stays in its own **territory** and works to keep other lions out of its area.

It's not easy being a lion cub. Cubs are the last to eat after a hunt. If food is hard to find, the adults eat, and the cubs go without a meal. When food is especially **scarce**, many cubs starve to death. Cubs are easy prey for some animals, such as hyenas, who think a lost cub is a tasty meal. When a lioness leaves to hunt or climbs a tree to get some rest, she hides her cubs under a bush or in the long grass. Sometimes, one lioness in the pride watches the cubs while the others go on a hunt.

Big Daddy

Male lions play with their own cubs and are very patient with them, but they do not like cubs that belong to other lions! When a male lion takes over a pride, he often tries to kill all of the cubs that live in the group and start his own family. Lion life is rough!

Quick Lift

A lion cub has a fold of skin on the back of its neck, just like a kitten. A lioness picks up her cubs by holding this skin gently in her teeth. It doesn't hurt the cub at all!

Baby File

Birth

A lioness leaves the pride when it is time for her to give birth to her cubs. Her **litter** may have two to five cubs, each one about the size of a small pet cat. The newborn cubs cannot see or walk, so their mother feeds and protects them. The cubs learn to walk when they are ten days old. When they are steady on their legs, their mother introduces them to the pride.

Three Months

Lion cubs are born with spotted fur, which helps to camouflage them. When they are about three months old, they lose their spots, and their pink noses start to turn black. Soon, the cubs begin to eat meat from animals their mother kills. They drink her milk until they are about eight months old.

One Year

Cubs learn to hunt when they are one year old. By the age of one, they are the size of big dogs. At age two, the males have manes. At three years old, the cubs are fully grown.

Life in the Pride

Female lion cubs usually stay with the pride forever. Male lions leave the pride when they are about three years old. The male lions roam around alone or with a small group of other single males until they are fully grown and ready to join a new pride. To join a pride, they chase away the male lions that are already in the pride. Then they mark their new territory by spraying **urine** around the land they want to take over. By marking their territory, they send a signal to any other lions in the area — stay away or risk a fight. A lion that does not pay attention to territory marks or warning roars may be killed.

Dividing the Work

It's the job of the male lions to protect the pride and patrol their territory for any lion that is not part of the pride. To help them chase away strangers, they have shaggy manes, which make them look big and scary, and they have a loud roar. While the males guard the territory, the females do most of the hunting. No matter which lion kills the prey, the males still get the first bite of meat.

Roar Facts

In the morning and in the evening, male lions walk out into their territory to roar. The sound of their roars is so loud, it can be heard for a long distance. They roar to let any other lions know who is the top cat in the area! Lionesses roar, too. Females roar to scare **predators** and to attract **mates**.

Watch Out!

Even while they are drinking, young lions keep a lookout for tasty snacks and enemies, such as hyenas!

Favorite Foods

Lionesses are the main hunters in the lion family. They go out early in the morning or at night to look for animals to eat. When a lioness spots her prey, she creeps close to it. She moves carefully so her prey does not see or hear her. When she is about 65 feet (20 meters) away — about the length of five cars — she breaks into a run. She pounces on her prey, killing it with one swipe of her paw or a bite to the neck.

Sharing the Kill

When a lioness makes a kill, she shares the feast with other lions in her pride. A big animal, such as a wildebeest or a large zebra, can keep a whole pride fed for a few days.

Teamwork

A group of lionesses must work together to catch big animals, such as zebras. Some of the lionesses hide in the long grass near the zebras. A few others walk around the zebra herd to attack from other sides. All at once, some lionesses leap out and chase the zebras toward the lionesses that are still hiding in the grass.

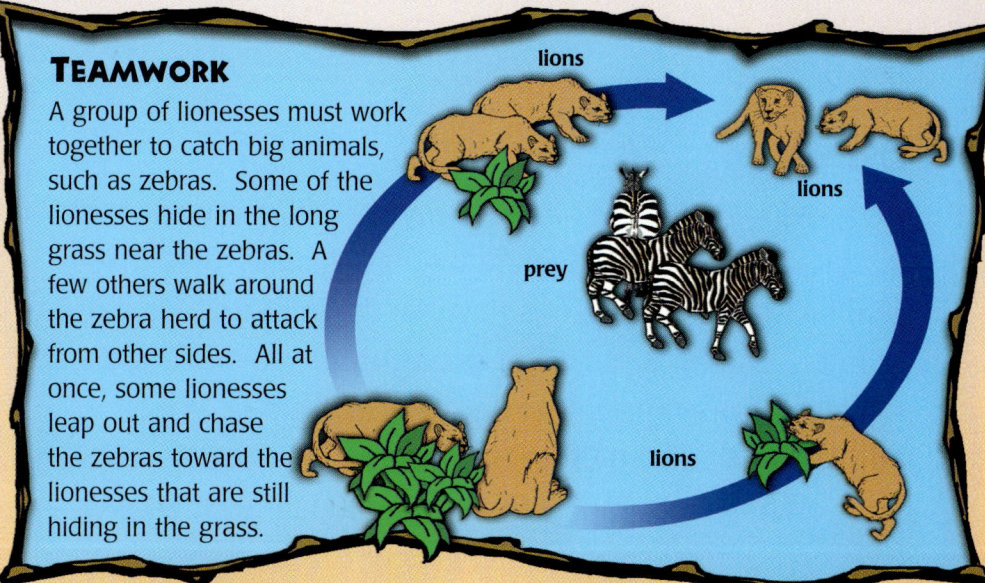

Playtime

Just like a pet kitten, a lion cub practices its hunting skills when it plays. First, its mother flicks her tail to help her cub learn to pounce. Later, cubs chase and pounce on their brothers, sisters, and cousins. As the cubs grow older, play gets rougher. Lions start hunting for real when they are two years old. Pet cats start hunting at a younger age, when they are about six months old.

Meaty Menu

The five favorite foods of lions are:
- wildeebeests
- buffaloes
- antelopes
- gazelles
- warthogs

Lions also like to eat:
- young giraffes
- young hippos
- young rhinos
- zebras

For a quick snack, lions grab:
- snakes
- squirrels
- birds
- hares
- lizards

Danger!

Full-grown lions do not have many animal enemies. Few animals even try to challenge a lion — usually they just steal the lion's food. Lions have far more to fear from the weather. During a period of **drought**, the savanna grass dries up. The animals that eat the grass die or leave to look for food elsewhere, which means that lions have fewer animals to hunt. Lions must compete with other savanna hunters, such as cheetahs and wild dogs. Lions may even have to eat animals that have already died, while vultures circle overhead and hyenas lurk nearby.

Sneak Thief!

Hyenas are sometimes called "laughing hyenas," but there is nothing friendly-looking about them. They have crooked legs, mean faces, and a horrible smell. Their coats are rough, and they look dirty. Hyenas are scavengers, which means they feed on dead animals and any meat they can steal from other animals. They often try to pester and distract lions so they can grab part of a kill. Sometimes hyenas even challenge lions to fights over food. Hyenas are not the only food thieves on the savanna. Lions steal meals from hyenas, too!

Danger Overhead!

As soon as lions make a kill, flocks of vultures start to circle in the sky. Vultures are large birds, but they do not hunt for their own food. Instead, these scavengers swoop down and try to steal some scraps away from a group of lions.

People Power

Lions' most dangerous enemies are humans. For thousands of years, people have killed lions and chased them off their land. Now, only about fifty thousand lions are left in Africa, and the number of Asiatic lions is less than one thousand. Hunting lions for sport is still allowed in some African countries. People also kill lions because they are afraid the lions will attack their families and their farm animals.

A Lion's Day

At sunrise, I woke up and walked off for my morning roar. With that job done, I settled down and went back to sleep.

One of the cubs woke me up. I yawned, stretched, and dozed again. I like to get about twenty hours of rest every day.

It isn't easy to sleep with cubs around. The youngest cub kept biting my tail. I don't mind her playful attacks. She will make a good hunter some day.

The cubs settled down to drink milk from their mother, so I got a little peace and quiet.

I decided to nap in the shade of an acacia tree. In mid-morning, it starts to get very hot out here on the savanna. I don't usually move from the shade until the weather cools down.

Noon is the hottest part of the day — and the quietest. All of the sensible animals are resting. I snoozed in my favorite tree.

I walked to the **water hole** for a drink. The lionesses say this is a good hunting spot.

6:00 PM — The sun set, and darkness settled in quickly. Lions are lucky to have very good eyesight in the dark, so we can still find our way around.

7:00 PM — The lionesses started to plan their night's hunting. I don't join in. My job is to patrol our territory while they're away. I don't want any other male lions coming near my pride!

8:00 PM — I went to the top of the hill and gave a good roar. That should scare away any lion that wanders into my territory.

9:00 PM — The lionesses took us to their kill. They were lucky tonight and caught a zebra without too much trouble. I ate first, of course. Then all the lionesses took their share. The cubs had to wait for the adults to finish.

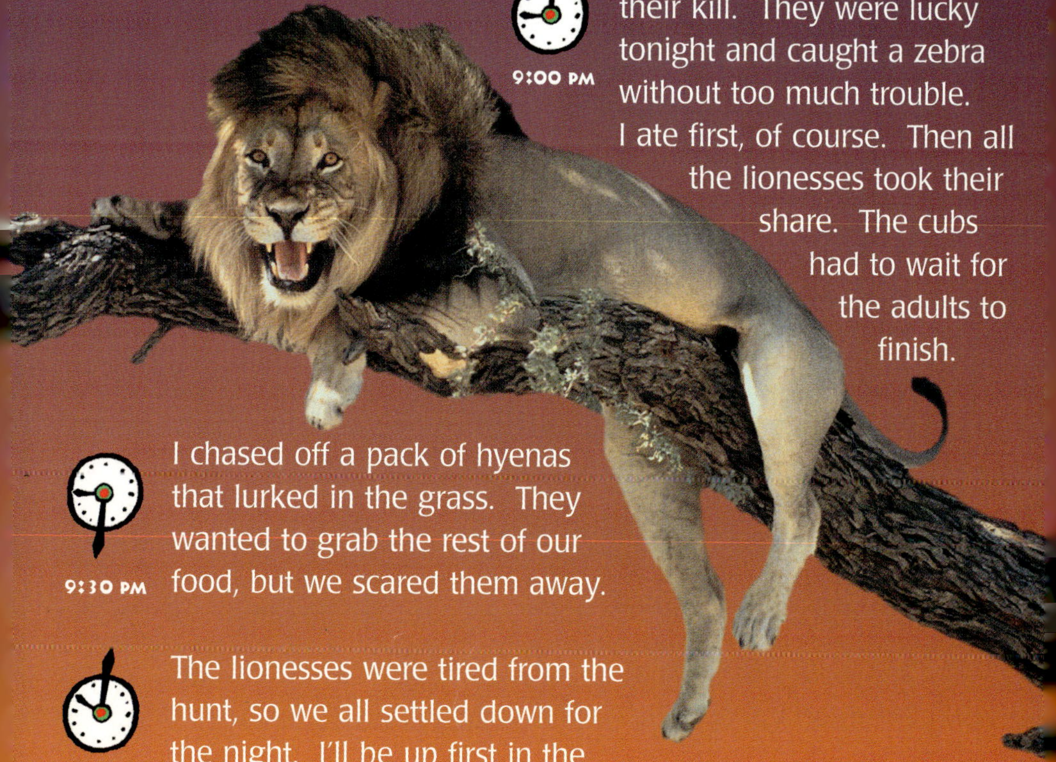

9:30 PM — I chased off a pack of hyenas that lurked in the grass. They wanted to grab the rest of our food, but we scared them away.

10:00 PM — The lionesses were tired from the hunt, so we all settled down for the night. I'll be up first in the morning to get the day started with a loud roar!

Relatives

Lions belong to the cat family. All cats are alike in many ways. They have good eyesight and hearing and a keen sense of smell. They all have sharp teeth and prefer to eat meat from animals that they have killed themselves. The members of the cat family walk quickly and quietly and often stalk their prey before pouncing. They are excellent hunters. Most big cats, such as lions, tigers, jaguars, and leopards, are able to do one thing that small cats, such as **domestic cats**, cannot do. Most of the big cats can roar.

Name Game

A wild cat found in North and South America goes by many different names. When people from Europe first saw it, they thought it was a lion that had lost its mane, so they called it a mountain lion. This cat is also called a puma, cougar, catamount, which is short for "cat of the mountain," mountain screamer, Indian devil, and purple feather!

Cheetah Chaser

Lions are called leaping cats because they sneak up on their prey and then pounce. Cheetahs are cats, too, but they are called running cats. Cheetahs run fast enough to catch animals such as zebras. In fact, cheetahs run faster than any other land animal over a short distance. They sprint at speeds of 62 miles (100 km) per hour!

Wild Cats in Africa

Lions aren't the only cats in Africa. Here are a few others:

- leopards
- cheetahs
- servals
- African wild cats
- caracals
- African golden cats
- black-footed cats
- sand cats

Did You Know?

Sea lions are definitely not lions, but they are like big cats in some ways. Sea lions eat meat and have hairy coats and whiskers. They also can roar. Some types of male sea lions even have manes!

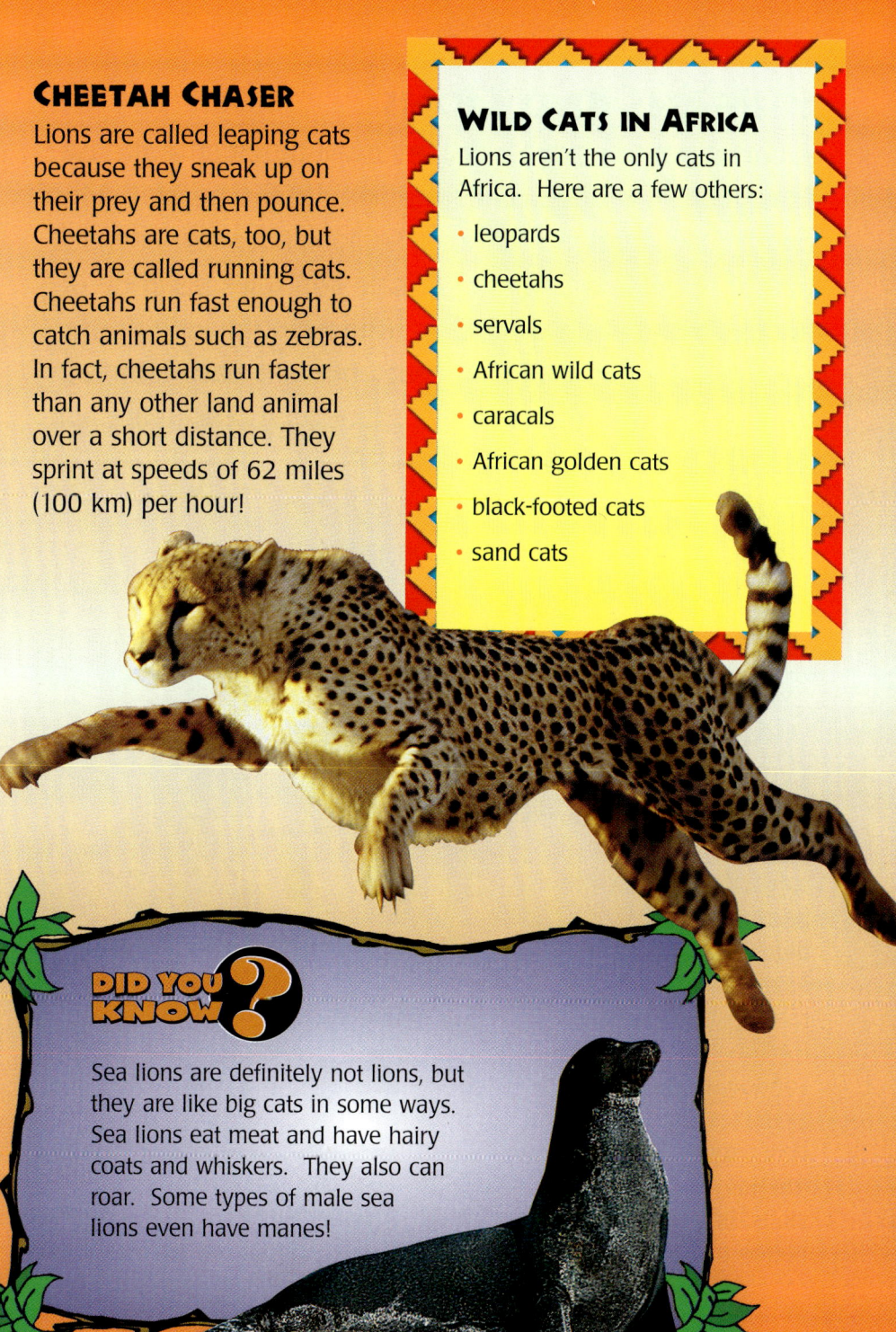

Humans and Lions

A lion is not the biggest or the fastest member of the cat family, but it is often called the "king of the beasts." Most people and animals fear lions, so lions have few enemies except humans with guns. A male lion rules his pride of lionesses and struts around as if he were the king of the savanna. For thousands of years, humans have admired the lion's power and strength. Many kings chose the lion as their royal symbol. In ancient Egypt, some of the great kings, called pharaohs, kept lions as pets! Other ancient people believed lions were gods.

London Lions

Many artists and sculptors love to use lions as subjects for their work because lions are so beautiful. A man named Edwin Landseer made bronze statues of lions for Trafalgar Square in London, England (*right*). In the Ice Age, millions of years ago, this spot was the home of real lions! Lions died out here long before the city was built.

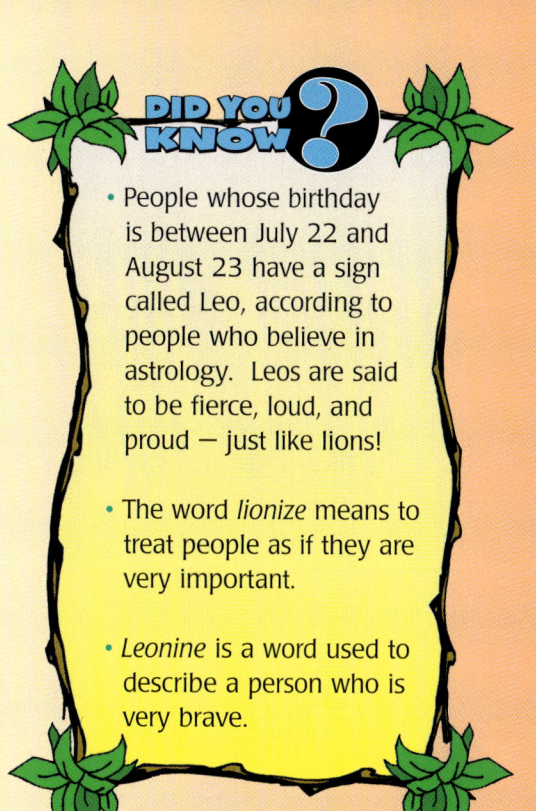

DID YOU KNOW?

- People whose birthday is between July 22 and August 23 have a sign called Leo, according to people who believe in astrology. Leos are said to be fierce, loud, and proud — just like lions!

- The word *lionize* means to treat people as if they are very important.

- *Leonine* is a word used to describe a person who is very brave.

Gone Wild

Hundreds of years ago, some hunters brought back strange animals from distant lands for other people to see. Wealthy people started their own zoos full of amazing animals. At first, people kept wild animals in cramped cages and forced them to do tricks. People now know that big animals such as lions live longer in places that give them plenty of space to roam. To watch lions in their natural surroundings, people often go on a **safari** or visit a **game reserve**.

Glossary

Acacia
A small tree or shrub that has feathery leaves and clusters of white or yellow flowers.

Baobab
A wide-trunked tree with fruit that looks like a gourd and bark used to make paper, cloth, and rope.

Camouflage
A color, pattern, or appearance that helps an animal blend in with its surroundings.

Carnivores
Animals that eat meat.

Cub
The young of some types of animals, including lions.

Domestic Cats
Cats that are no longer wild but are kept as pets.

Drought
A long period of very dry weather. Rivers dry up, and the grass turns brown and dies.

Game Reserve
An area of land set aside as a place where wild animals and plants can live in their natural surroundings without being disturbed or harmed by humans.

Gazelles
Antelopes of a type known for grace and speed. Gazelles are found in Africa and Asia.

LITTER
A group of young born to one mother at the same time.

MATES
Animal partners that come together to produce or raise young.

POUNCE
To jump on top of something suddenly and unexpectedly.

PREDATORS
Animals that hunt other animals for food.

PREY
Animals that another animal hunts and kills for food.

SAFARI
A trip, often in Africa, to see, photograph, or hunt wild animals.

SCARCE
Rare and hard to find.

SPINES
Sharp, pointed growths, such as thorns or quills, on some types of plants and animals.

TERRITORY
A large area of land claimed by someone or something for a particular use.

URINE
An animal's liquid waste.

WATER HOLE
A natural hole or low-lying area that holds water.

Index

Africa 10, 11, 23, 27
Asiatic lions 10, 23

camouflage 12, 17
claws 7
cubs 9, 14, 16, 17, 18, 21, 24, 25

ears 8, 9
enemies 8, 19, 22, 23, 28
eyesight 8, 9, 25, 26

fighting 8, 18, 22
food 9, 16, 21, 22, 23, 25
fur 6, 9, 11, 17

game reserves 29

hair 6, 27
heads 7, 8
hearing 8, 9, 26
humans 8, 10, 23, 28, 29
hunting 8, 11, 16, 17, 18, 20, 21, 22, 23, 24, 25, 26

jaws 7, 8, 9

legs 6, 17, 22
lionesses 9, 14, 16, 17, 19, 20, 21, 24, 25, 28

male lions 6, 8, 14, 16, 17, 18, 19, 25, 28
manes 6, 8, 17, 18, 26, 27

paws 7, 20
playing 16, 21, 24
pouncing 6, 20, 21, 26, 27
predators 19
prey 6, 7, 8, 9, 11, 16, 18, 20, 26, 27
prides 14, 16, 17, 18, 20, 25, 28

roaring 18, 19, 24, 25, 26, 27
running 6, 27

safaris 29
savannas 10, 11, 12, 13, 22, 24, 28
scavengers 22, 23
sleeping 24

tails 6, 21, 24
teeth 8, 9, 17, 26
territories 14, 18, 19, 25
tongues 9

water hole 24
whiskers 8, 27